The Greenwood Poet

Lancelot Schaubert

‡

Copyright © 2022 by Lancelot Schaubert
All rights reserved.

This is a work of fiction. Names, characters, places, and incidents either are the product of the author's imagination or are used fictitiously, and any resemblance to actual persons, living or dead, business establishments, events, or locales by name or by likeness is entirely coincidental.

   Schaubert, Lancelot
   The Greenwood Poet / Lancelot Schaubert
   ISBN-13: 978-1-949547-06-1
   1. POETRY / Subjects & Themes / Death, Grief, Loss
   2. FICTION / Romance / Historical / Regency
   3. FICTION / Fairy Tales, Folk Tales, Legends & Mythology
   I. Greenwood Cemetery (New York)
   II. Brooklyn (New York)
   Printed in the United States of America

FACTS TO KEEP IN MIND :

Assumptions to keep in mind before reading these poems:

1. I grew up poor and among relatively uneducated folk of mixed heritage (Gaelic Catholic, Yiddish German, German Lutheran, Cherokee, Blackfoot, some Roma -- a blend of what others call "white trash" or "the yellow people"), therefore I've never taken a poetry class. This has freed me to do some things with form often forgotten in the MFA and theology wings of most colleges and literary magazines. Certainly it gives me a perspective on how the poor view poetry, for the folk song and the hip hop stanza have always remained alive and well, whatever everyone else says of the death of poetry. The poor and ignorant know meter, verse, and rhyme even when they can't articulate what they're doing. Yet those folk love the land and its animals like St. Francis and Fred Danback and Chesterton and Noah. They know all the magic names of Brother Sun and Sister Water, Brother Fire and Sister Fawn.

3. I moved to Brooklyn in 2014. For all of my friends and neighbors talk of the letter of the

law of eco-friendly, zero-wasteful, sustainable life, most seem woefully unconnected to the land, the lesser beasts, their siblings in bark. I believe this is largely due to the materialist or analytic philosophy undergirding all they do: ecology, for them, is all about efficiency and material causation. Progress, it seems, does not apply to the undergirding moral law and metaphysics that would make it easier for them to save the planet.

4. Meanwhile many of my friends at home in Southern Illinois and Missouri seem unable to draw a clean line from their alleged neoplatonic faith and the passionate conservation pioneered by their conservative hero Theodore Roosevelt, who started the national park program. They seem dead-set on privatizing national parks, a policy that would benefit none of them and would likely benefit only oil barons, rich bankers, and coastal elites capable of buying up said land. Conservatism, it seems, does not apply to conserving the planet referred to in the hymn they sing: *This is My Father's World.*

5. Weary and wary of this, I now walk three blocks up from my apartment to Greenwood

Cemetery to regularly pray in their chapel, sit by the cherry blossoms in the water, put bare feet on clean grass, rest against brother sycamore and sister willow, meditate, and write poetry. I write one every time I go and I've noticed some things. For one, runners and pets and sports are unwelcome. For another, it's the realm of the dead and half the city's superstitious and the other half fears facing their coming death and the circumstances which shall attend their death. As a result, it's empty almost always. And so I keep the dead company alongside a living and breathing biosphere, goose and goosebuster, bay fig and birdwatcher, snake and sonnet, tree and tower in the background when viewed from the highest point in the cemetery (the highest point in Brooklyn). It's interesting because the high places were places of worship, historically. Some attracted barrows as ours has. Some attracted heretical human sacrifice and sex cults (the prostitute of the epic of Gilgamesh, and Zeus's jealous wives, come to mind). Some, first owned by counts who heard great preaching, ended up gifted to the likes of St. Francis. What do you give to a prayerful monk who took a vow of poverty?

Answer: a mountain. Where he can pray.

That in mind, the more I meditate on Greenwood Cemetery, the more I see the trees sending out shoots into the rest of the land and world to remind it what it has otherwise attempted to imprison behind the black gates. I see spores and seeds and husks and pollens leaving the hills and barrows and seeding themselves in the cracks of tower and tin lizzy and television screen. I hear fresh wind blowing from leaf and lake to scatter smog.

We attempted to jail her, but Sister Nature will not go quietly.

For she and not we holds the keys to the gates.

We thought ourselves the jailers. We've turned out to be a large, mutually-complicit chain gang who have, like some dark Peter and James and John, built tents to make permanent our chains, walling and barring ourselves in with our machinations.

Sister Nature stands at the cellblock door and knocks. For the dead are not those dwelling in her tombs.

Lancelot Schaubert
Green-wood Cemetery
Brooklyn
2021

GREENWOOD'S PORTCULLIS

We seem as we come to see, we are
As we're metaphoring, making our symbols.
Decisions decide seldom our fates,
But seeing is believing and so being,
By training tears how to tunnel to the core
Of our being by certain symbols we make
Convictions and they change vitals on the screen
Till the heart beats heathen drums
Over the dell, arming militias
With parishes and priests, prepping locals
With the Unknown God's embers in the hearth
Of the nearest inn, newest hut,
Closest cloister. If our current basic
Images of self undercut the cosmic
In our house and heather, how will we be?
Whom shall I bewilder but me?

For this the thistles and theater of the graves
And barrows beckon: by my street
Stands the last castle of loving Fae.
The black gates blind us to the true
Borders of the realm. Bystanders point
To their midnight walks and the masked coons

>   Locked inside. Late night guards
>   Are making the rounds, managing mischief
> 30 And thank God for the thick fence
>   That keeps out the kids. Curious how they
> miss it...
>
>   The Castle of the Fae calls us home.
> 35 Hear in the heart of harrowing stone
>   And bone and steel and brazen calves
>   With the moneyed masses of maybe five
>   Percent of the city sure in their millions.
>   The White Horse wonders at the fall from
> 40 Across the pond's chasm and hopes:
>
>   Greenwood gapes, its grapes await
>   The press to empty, to pass away
>   The age of ink, aching to fill
> 45 Her with grapes again. If you get here early
>   And hold still, you'll hear Fae come
>   When the traffic stills, trains hush and
>   Planes quiet: on the prickle of hawthorn,
>   In the splash of the fountain, displayed in
> 50 blades
>   Of greenwood grass: greet the tiniest armies
>   Of the hoards of heaven hiding though tall,
>   Diminished though mighty, demeaned to use
>   Superstition as their safety net

55 And the black gates to blind the masses.
They hide in here. Hear them whisper:

*"Oh family in Forbes, oh friends in canyons,
Oh the Amazon eaters: we're eager to see*
60 *Mankind surrender their many screens
And see again, seem the image,
Become the metaphor that's calling their being."*

65 We are as we come to clearly see.
And we see seldom the sylphs in the trees
Twittering and singing the truth of the boughs
We think we protect with thistle and cage
70 And the black gates that bind graves.

But it's the outer edge of unearthly kingdoms
We may never meet or know
Because of phones. Because of bad sight.
75 Because the light has been carried from our eyes
Into artificial asteroids and stars
In our personal box, private Pandoras
By the millions while Mind diminishes in The
80 West.

We are what we come to clearly see.
Image emerges at the end of our hearts,
We become that and claim no more.

85

But the black gate hides a buried Welcome
Mat under the ivy if you search.
Seek and find. Sing and hear.

The River Runs

    When the tide turns
    And the river runs home
    You will know
    That in one way only
    Can salt water and fresh water flow from the same spring
    When the tide turns
    And the river runs home
    Fresh current collides with the high moon's salt.

    St. Paul: he meant profanity and praise
    Bless words and curse words
    Ought not come out your mouth
    This the man who counts it all shit to know Christ
    This the disciple of Moses
    Who read
    Bless words and curse words
    Across the two mountains
    The one we follow as he follows
    Jesus who called Herod a whiny little
    Female fox
    The new Elijah who
    Mocked the prophets of Baal whose
    god was on the shitter

When the tide turns
And the river runs home
You will know in one way only
Can salt water and fresh water flow from the same mouth

For it takes blue language to incarnate gospel
Inside the mechanic's shop
That he may be saved on his own terms
In his own terms

terms and conditions apply:

Paul would be cut off for the sake of his own people
Jesus descended into hell
Love condescends
Says Orpheus

For praise to incarnate
In the language of curse
So that the curse becomes blessing

It's the addict
Experiencing homelessness

55 Who looks at me once it clicks:

"Holy shit Jesus Chris is fucking awesome. This is real?"
"This is real."
60
They overfished the oysters in the Hudson
And the lack of salty meat
Let in the storm
Let in
65 *Sandy.*

We needed the tide to turn.
We needed the life of the flesh where the saltwater and freshwater meet
70 Where only the squirming sea life lives
For them
The river runs home

Gilded by Greenwood

In the tower I saw tumbling drops
Obscure skies and scour the air
Of its acid atoms, the atom bomb's
Rain's making, realizing climate
Change is carbon in the clear midair
And a flying flood, flails from the heavens
Would drain slower. So dreary to thrive
Skyward away from the scalding drenched
Greenwood stones, the gold splashing
And muddy mashing molded for the dregs
Of society's grapes. See the corner
Room of the hotel? Rays whiten,
Brighten walls while brooms sweep
In the dark quarters, daylight on one
And clouds on the other. Clearly Van Gogh
Knew that the Kirke could claim the light
Again if the good in the great world
Would spin from the windows of spritely
Christians
And spinning down the spray of rain
On the Unknowing Arms of New Yorkers
Instead of staying stuck and conserved.

In the tower teem tumbling drops,
Rains beget rains, rights beget beauties,
And exposing your pride to the painful goods

is the only way to open the sky
     To be scoured of demons by showers of light:

30
     The good of Greenwood could gild your
blankets.

Glaciers and their Graves

    Of great glaciers and their graves in the waters
       In the deep of the waves, dead in the heat,
       Which millennia loved to labor from snow
       And how the hells happened to melt
       Their histories from the earth and the heavens away --
       These the thinking thunders and women
       Grieve as the ghosts of the greatest of men:
       Ice and Hector, Arthur and snow
       Are the lingering lives of the long-forgotten
       Forged Foundations -- *Oh Fountains of Cold!* --
       that held back the heat from the heavens and earth
       To hold in the hells that the hard ice
       Had put to a slumber, prison of winter,
       Beneath the surface, next to the sea
       Of the Transantarctic tunnels and peaks.

    The monsters had claimed to have made our earth
       As a punchline to a joke, power as humor:

       What was our first wild creature
       To go into space? *The great cow*

Who easily jumped over the moon.

30 We may be cattle to monsters and the elder
    Things and shoggoths, but think of whether
    They themselves are thaumaturges
    Great enough to give themselves
    The being they bear: brightness, how does it
35 Linger in their eyes, how's the light writhing?
    Oh can they... can they cause themselves?
    And if *théy* are contingent, think of the glaciers...

40 Of great glaciers and their graves in the waters
    In the deep of the waves, dead in the heat,
    Which millennia loved to labor from snow
    And how the hells happened to melt
45 Their histories from the earth and the heavens away --
    How Being donates to -- bar none --
    Every contingent entity
    And the grace of the glaciers that was given
50 once
    May one day waken and find
    Its power to bind those eldritch things
    Has returned to tame, totally frozen
    As a fortunate thing, a fearsome chill

55   Both awful and awesome, early in the morning
       The rise of Winter's revenant morn,
       The soul of the cold that stars great
       Saves and softens so the searable things
60   May grow green and gift life:

       Of great glaciers and their grace in the waters,
       How mist freezes, may unthaw,
65   Might lighten, might be ice
       Again and again if the good of it returns:

       Hardened and hardy, here to guard,
       And happy to hold in the heat of our doom,
70   And happy to hold in the heart of our darkness,
       And happy to hold in the hells of the cosmos:

       Again and again, glaciers return.

The River Roots First

    The pond by the tombs was punctured and drained
    Into the echo of the aquifer
5   And it burst and blanket the boundless heights
    Of the deep dark to don some old
    Island's archipelago and the East River
    Forms flying far to the north
10   Splitting hillsides and sowing Greenwood
    In the crags and crusts the crews blast
    But whose bridges flaccid barely lasted
    The weekend rust, weakened, untrusted,
    The memory of man. Makes lunches
15   Of urban centers, eating the civic,
    Returning towers to time's flowers--
    Grass growing in groves on crags,
    Steel to slags and our summerings to ice.

20   We stack stones, stealing from the vista
    Of mountains unmade in the morning upstate,
    Creatures -- crags -- cry to the sky
    And summon their songs of circlets and
25   orbits.

    The leak leaves to loam stones

And bring bones to beach stone
Statues like marbles or strands of beach glass,
Everest to Epcot by the evening spray
Of Greenwood's waters and the grey of the thing
Who could be dead. It can't quite take.

North and north and near the back
Of Boreas hides the blame of day,
The path of the grace to the pool risen
And the nonentity of nobles and rich--
Upstate... well it isn't a second home.
The river and groves root here first.

Union Called Him Captain Hook

Gunpowder fog
His Evinrude emits.
Sun dots its "i"
Shoreline crosses green "t"
Orange and baby blue gilding
My father
In a busted down Ranger fishing boat
Having pulled me behind him
-- Until the waters whipped me
Black and blue
At sixty miles an hour on the golden arc
Barrel roll body
Apparently water can wrack testicles prior to whiplash.
This I did not know.

It's calm now
In my father's wake
We have few years left
But we respect drawn lines
A rooster tail shoots up between us
A late good speed
He docks along
And fades back towards
Circular fire
And the smoke of his enemy's

Cannon fire.
His death will beg the bards to weep.
30   At least this one.

The Power of Italian Agronomy

The Italy of Europe and its Union erodes
Like marble stones. Mind the cracks
BnBs booked over the Air
Whipsawed through wind in wood beam
And stone seam. Sirs and daughters,
Sons and madams searching the country
For a home or a hearth hiding in the farms,
An urban to rural umbrage for pilgrims
Once sent so west that they settled there
And birthed babies in Brooklyn (as they had
In Sicily) as soon as they saw The Lady.

Reminds me of the Merry Christma--
--Stravaganza that struck a chord:
The Oh Hellos off in an old blinding
Manger and Mundis melody of joy
Over the ears of almost pilgrims
Blood faced and black necked
By Christmas lights. Caroling loud,
Persuaded to sing, spurred to worship.

We wander. Watch our earnings
Chase us asunder. Chance plays such a
Small role in smiting our chances:
It's greed's grip on growing things.

26 ‡ The Greenwood Poet

But cauliflower still pierces stone.

THE PROBLEM WITH GROWING THINGS

The Greenwood grows, gains in the spirit
Of Providence's priming, pruning the vines,
Climbs cleanly and cleaves the steel
I-beams and each armored truck
And concrete block, captivating Manhattan
By the tanglewood of thundering Brooklyn,
Cracked marble, creased highways,
Root thunders and breaks new roads:

I'm seated among the rich, certain elites
Of city center, seeing their weeding,
Their breeding attempts to banish shoots
And shoot the shit about green leaves
They made grey and marbled yellow.
They wield herbicide, overlooking
How they're dying, they are the dead
In these catacombs. Calling to me
In the morning as I rise to make poems,
Calling, "Copy *our* copy, writer."

I am in labor. Love-making
Impregnated me with poetry and I swelled
For nine months. New language
Is forcing its way through my five holes,
Tearing things. Teaching these Mad Men:

Greenwood grows, glows in the cracks
Of the archipelago, eating pains
To shit light where the shame should go--
It knows what we need, nestled green
Where rust creeps, running the schemes
of ruin and wrath and beckons with disease
By growing things. Greenwood thrives
In the wings of the world by wing-seeding.
Word-seething. Whittling verse
And wakening song and unweeding
Concrete playgrounds that cultivate the famous.

Dusting Greenwood Chapel's Marble

There's grass inside the chapel, on the stone,
The marble evidence of what was mowed.
It scattered, sacrament of common time
And messes up the white, the walls of bone.
The hand-carved rails, green marble, scarlet seats,
A birthday present's leavings: trim and bows.
The maintenance man arrives to blow the leaves
And fresh-cut grass from alcove, nook, and grime.
The sound afflicts the chapel with a charge
To face the tech, to land, collide with barge.

But grass on marble is the chapel's heart,
For grass and prayer's where chapels get their start
And so I filled the truck the man had brought
With sod and seed and sapling grafted, wrought,
I filled the floor and walls as best I could
To turn the inner church into Earth's wood.
Come see: the inside's bigger than the out

"Was always so," have claimed the most devout.

A Storm Assaults the Stained Glass of Greenwood Chapel

    The glass goes dark and the green field
    Behind the unhidden hope of the risen
    Fades from frame. The frames are black.
    The seams slacken and the sudden glories
    -- of the time my cousin took her life
    And the time my wife woke temper --
    When the words and signs in the windows
carried
    Me back to broken, born again
    And again and again in the gate of poems
    And prophetic furies. Funny how a snow
    Or a hard heavy heavenly raining
    Will erase the rumors you really wanted
    And replace their prose with the perfect
word:

    Stained glass seams. Sable cracks,
    Yet to seal the scenes. A surge and another
    hits the hues, how it soaks,
    Till the words in the window weep their
symbols:
    Rivers from "life," "resurrection" a wet thing.

    Even the early eaves of white

Chapel stonework can change their reflection
To the dark grey of dirge played
30 Light and lithe, and loam and stone
Is readied for the rising of ruined buried
Things that grow grey there in the dark,
Light under heavy. Listen to the rain
Stuck in the glass, streams in the weeds,
35 Blood in the bones and breath in the dust.

Perugia Under Different Suns

    Shadows on slates. Shadows on grates,
    Then grating gravel that goes asphalt,
    Black then green -- blue peatmoss
    Like a pea tree dish placidly grows
    Or hillsides and old homes for the Fae
    In the woods of my youth whittled to scoops
    Of green gelato gripping so many
    Clay cups halved -- then clear skies
    Murk up a bit, making the born
    Go grey a sec. Gone once more,
    Shadow on stucco stippled walls
    Bound by claws of brown iron,
    Massive legs from Mecha Chickens
    Shoved like spikes in the sheer by two
    Large climbers. Did little children
    Build this of split blocks of Legos --
    Marble, but Legos? Mortar slathered
    On the cake batter, cracked, frosting,
    Green shutters -- grey, yellowed --
    From a western set?

                       Weakened   from
Quakes,
    Threatened by storms, could be torched or
melted.

But it lingers, the light, and lounges over nooks
And cradles crannies, crafting the way
To illuminate lost corners
Of the great hollows in the glowing town.

Shade is not a thing. Shade isn't light
But where weather has wakened and moved
To some long lost illumination
And its subtle source: how shining the light
Becomes land and love, liquid and air,
Mammal and mollusk, mercury and dragon,
Woman and man, weapon and the castles
That predicate the walls and powdered black:

Slates and grates, slaves and gravel:
The shapes of light when shouldering shadows.

Perugia from a Balcony

For salt they split and warred how we for tea
And postage taxes killed our families.
For long enough their fratricide endured
Until they hired the Swiss to fight the Swiss.

The slates of clay will break and fly amiss
And shoot as sleds of dogs on frozen, pure,
Albedo snow -- the moss on slate and stone
Invokes Miss Nature over marble, brick,
And patches piercing into layered slacks
Of towers's legs like armor, sculpture, bones.

Sashiko stitches bind my bride's release:

What predicates our patchwork wars but peace?

PRESENCE

      I know the sunning secret
      Of the dying of the phones --
      The natural consequences --
5   The quest from lone to Lone.

      I've held their shackles processors
      Their sparkles little husks
      And smiled across the table
10   At my bearded friend, his musk.

      I've witnessed acts of treachery
      And tasted molten silk
      And other things once caged by rings
15   Of phones -- hot tea and milk.

      For some, they called me from afar --
      My lifeless phone in hand
      While present with me Papa tucked
20   His toes in Coney's sand.

      I've missed a many telegraph.
      I rarely phone it in.
      I've ghosted texts, gone straight to voicemail
25   --
      Every telesin.

But I can say this over brunch
Because damn phone is dead.
For I am not a cyborg
Or an internet in head.

I'm presently your person.
I'm here while you are here.
I've nowhere on my lifeless phone
Found answers to my fears:

That I will die still childless,
That I will meet abyss,
That I will fail at writing,
That this is my last kiss:

But there without distraction
In the teeth of every void
I make and love and make my love
Till hell itself's annoyed.

FOR A HEART OF GOLD

I dumped the sun at dawn in the Hudson
Where the fountainhead first flings tears.
You'd think such a thing would thunk like a
ball,
Headlong splash, harrowing wake,
But the sun sank slower than driftwood,
Than small rocks. Sliding out the globe
The molten gold magma goes,
The nukes and novas and neoplasms --
Pitcher and juice -- so the Prime Matter
Of the river's form renders alchemical
Magnum opus -- the molten fountain
To the dark delta drains as the light
Of the winter morning washing the city --
Gold glows and goes with the flow,
Smelting the waters, gilding the blue.
Blind me, waves, and bind sight
To the white gold washing south
As the day darkens, deem the hope
Ready for New Yorkers, righten the wrongs.
Manhattan Midas make us more than stocks,
Philosopher's stone leave us better
And longing for the mouth where the light
moves
And leaks back into lordly black
Being in void, birthing in the womb

Of the world's pain -- wakes carrying
Grateful and grumbling green on the vine
30   And the vine's thorns, verily the giraffe
Kicks her foal in the key thirty
Minutes at the start of mothering so the kid
Can learn how to run -- righting the boat
road
35   The liquid light leaks into the pitcher
Of dark and dusk, drawn in thrust
For the following day when fire will be called
Down from deity in the dirge of the spring
Upstate reborn over the wake
40   Of the pure waters. Pray for my seeking
For the gold getting isn't gain for me
But the being made brighter inside
Heart of gold, healed by light.

ANTI-REBELLION

"The next real literary 'rebels' in this country might well emerge as some weird bunch of anti-rebels."
— *David Foster Wallace*

Give me childish gall or give me death.
Give me my child's gall at the moment of her death.
In a chalice. Watered down with
Three-dollar wine.
Make my entendre take vows of celibacy.
Revere untrendy human troubles:
Idol idylls,
Enshrine sincere shriners
The big beer belly ones with the tiny jelly belly cars in the annual Little Egypt Parade.

Convict me of sadness.
Convict me of courage.
Do not convict me of a sad courage.
Only courageous sadness:
To be a man and to weep openly,
Grown ass tears in public streaming down
A muscled, bearded frame, or
An unmuzzled, clean-shaven cheek with its kamikaze attempt at poetry

Till death do we part.

"You have been charged, how do you plea?"
"I plead that I am happy, your honor."
"The court finds you guilty on all counts. Twenty years, no parole."
"They will be my happiest years, your honor."
"Are you being ironic? Are you making fun of me?"
"No, ma'am. I'm happy to go to prison for this, your honor. I deserve prison and prison will be a monastery for a man such as me."
"Are you mocking my honor?"
"No, ma'am, I believe You're Honor's your honor, your honor."

I ought not start writing such poems.
It'd be the death of me.
And my kids (see above).
And my poems: still
Births in the literary wing of the hospital
Oh wait, it has a heartbeat?
Post-birth abort it, then.
Oh wait, you resuscitated it?
Gas. Injections. Slay the little childer.
Too sincere, repressed, backward, quaint.

                Virgin-birth-naïve.

                Gollum, in his way and with more excuses
                (For brief acquaintance)
                Made the same mistake:
                Confusing kindness
                With blindness.

                Water-to-wine-naïve.

                Give me your yawns, your rolled eyes, your
                cool smile, your PBR, your bald-with-beards,
                your long-on-top, your feminine jeans that you
                don't quite remember whether it is a good or a
                bad that they're feminine anymore. Or if they
                still are feminine -- per se -- anymore -- you
                make them tighter, yes tighter for the girls:
                leggings, please, you beg. Let pants fade into
                non-pantity. Make panty pants. Panting, you
                thirsty un-rational animal, you. And now yawn
                after feasting. Roll your eyes. Cold blooded
                smile. Give me your huddled hipsters. Not the
                external kind. The seen-it-all, done-it-all, don't-
                mean-shit kind. I lift my lamppost beside the
                wardrobe door:

Are you ready you non-pardox? You tertium-quidless binary? You unironic irony? Poor hollowed out thing?

85 Give me banality or give me death.
Give me banality that gives me death.
Give me, give me, give me my banal death.
Drought or drowning.
My death. Seriously, shut up and hand it over
90 right now. I want it back. Please. And thank you.
They're called the magic words.
Give me anxieties and pains and sufferings and whatever kind of death shall please Thee
Even now from thy hand, willingly and
95 cheerfully I receive it.
It's hilarious.
Dying.
(No irony. I mean it:
I scoff at this stingless boney thing.)
100 And give me liberty and give me death.
And give me the liberty of my death.
I receive thy child's gall. My child's gall. And the gall of her three-dollar wine.
Give me the heat death of the universe.
105 Give me the nonentity of fading science.
Give me the decay of art.

I lift my lamppost beside the wardrobe door:

110 Let it fade. Let it fade. Let it fade to black.
Let the black fade to nothing per se.
Let it really be a real Nothing.
Not black, not space, not time ticking.
Just nothing.
115
Then make it a real, live Nothing.

Then give me the Resurrection of all things,
Wake up whatever causes sleep. Real ones,
120 every one listed in the
Manifest.
I mean it.
I will not avert my gaze.
It's a staring contest. Double dare.
125 Look into my eyes. My born ogler's eyes.
My healed Tom Sawyer eyes.
My childish voyeurism with no lust in sight.

You blinked.
130
Or maybe I just see through you?
Maybe I see through you who see through everything?
You are not the means by which I

135   See tree and stock, rock and wave, heat and grave,
    Flame and flagon.
    Soil. And breath.
    Real things. Water never disgusts me.

140
    Oh you poor, poorrich littlebig nothingthing.
    What, do like dewdrop-laden morning grasses hurt your newly bare feet?
    Is gossamer now razor wire on those see-
145 through now-gloveless fingers of yours?
    Did mocking substance cap your bare knees?
    Is seeing through things making you see-through?

150   Most windows forget their sills these days.
    Very few glasses bear lenses.
    And fewer still remain ensilvered.

    But last of all?

155
    Only like three kaleidoscopes and four spyglasses remain.

Hornblower Waits on Pier 11

"City that Never Sleeps oh tell
Me when do you dream?" Whelp. She asked
It to a crowd of drunks, crying skunks,
And washed-up wannabe musicians
And them carrion eaters: cowardly producers
Who come to peck at wee creatures the
West weathered into such wonderful and seemly
Shapes and faces, sounds and forces,
Great guitar strums, green soundscapes,
Manuscripts in suitcases,
Cornbelt holes, said White, in their hearts.

Them and the agents, thinkers, and the grifters
Actors also hire, and the All Street
Babies who barely brandish a razor
Weekly pre-trade. What is it then?
Between us tryers? Tell me, brother:
Scores counted, centuries mounted
Wildly between us, Walt can you see?

The broken land, barely hills,
Was it yours in youth? Yet... still mine?

Your ferry flies to the future shores

Where I stand at the base of the sturdiest
bridge
30 The blood of our brothers and bloody
mothers
Brick by brick built with lives,
Looking back, longing not for me
Earlier or awesomer, but open to you,
35 Walt Whitman. Was of body --
Yours should be -- yearning forward
To me and mine, myth and time
Memorized and minded, but many or none.

40 I'll answer. I will meet
Your question and the yearning in hers:

For a city that never sleeps is deprived
Of the dreams in the dark that divinized
45 minds
Find freeing. So they freak when nightmæres
Rise in the river (rioting Hudson),
Walk in Wall Street and weather the fog:
It is a dreamscape dreary that we dream and
50 live,
For insomnia suffers a city of ghosts.

But we lucid dreamers lay hold of it.

55   Nightmæres release, neutered of forcing
        Themselves on me. See me here?

        Lucid dreamer. Lay hold of the
        Count of the scores, keep time with me,
60   Mark twain and measure twice:

        Walk, Whitman. Waltz in my dream,
        I in the poem, admirable approach, say
        Nighest name but never a word.
65   We flow with the flood-tide, frolic from shoresides
        To meet in the vale, mindless of Tors.

        Come to us on the waters. Cryn't. Lookn't
70   down.
        What is between? What is the count?

        Your nine stanzas.
                                    And now mine.
75

CAROL FOR CHARLOTTE CANDA

Charlie Canda, Napoleon's,
Came here eighteen-twenty-one
Sired Charlotte, daughter of the gun
Horses away, horses away!

At seventeen, a party threw.
Afterwards, escort her to
Another home, a friend, they knew
What's in the head of Charlotte

When Charlie came, his daughter's gone
As storm and lightning carried on
Down Broadway, carriage sang its song:
Horses away, horses away.

Careening round the corner came
Charlotte tossed by tossing manes
Out the carriage to what's paved
What's in the head of Charlotte?

Her dad arrived and mother too
And cradled in their hands who flew
She passed away. The steeds, they knew:
Horses away, horses away

They sketched her stone with rose and wreath
Interred at Pat's. Now there beneath
30   Her whitened fount you kneel on heath
And quietly there, her ghost bequeaths
What's in the head of Charlotte.

Horses away, horses away
35   *What's in the head of Charlotte.*

Leaf blower
Ushers the grass
From chapel

Your Brother's Blood Cries Out

Cold clings to the cropless streetlight
Planter that loudly preaches its name:
"Capital of the World when it Comes to
Finance,"
With pictures of towers pruned with a sunburst
Obscuring cold brick, scouring the real dawn.

You can forget how a great grappling or rappelling
Site iconic stands over
Your morning mischief. Memory of Kong's
Hanging have left. How could you still
Be under Chrysler when the evensong stills
In the sky's garden? In the skipped planter?

Greenwood whispers: "Get ye some seeds
In your high bowls. Heat ye this ice
And leak it inside. Lean the windows,
Bend the light from the bright layers
Twenty stories tall above
And help it hit your hardy chalice."

They line Third, longing for roots,
Longing for shoots in the shooting lanes

Where men still make meat of their brothers,
Yet now with nothing to needle with guilt:
30   For how can blood harp from the soil
When soil can't be seen in the streets of grey?

LITTLE BROTHERS, WHAT BLOOMS?

Oh what blooms, little brothers,
I didn't see you dodging notice
There on the glass, thick coffee
Table amid tracts of prayers:

On my intellect dense and dark, pour
Your brilliance and grant breakthrough here,
Penetrating, pensive mind,
Retentive memory, method to learn...

What learning have you, little brothers?
What memory makes your many leaves
Reach for the stars? Righting stems?
Seeding sprouts? Sunned and carboned?

I touch your dirt, tangleroot and spongy,
Full of shit, firey microbes,
The thing that thugs thinking of racing
Dragstrip cars drain on the pistons.
The soil smiles, shirks, and whispers
Of the worms of the dead that wake Greenwood.
Memento mori, method to live:
That I will die but one way,
Why worry on which version

Shall take me away? *Tolle lege.*

30 Cities that run from certain death
Tend to build tombs for apartments
And hide the worms, hush the plants.
Oh what blooms, little brothers,
I didn't see you dodging notice
35 There on the dead, thin sands.

Glass gives space: grave prayers.

Elegy for a Star

    In Greenwood Cemetery on the grass
    I laid and baked beneath our local Star
    And thought of how I claimed that she
5 would pass
    From cupping hands into Sir Hudson's heart.
    How trite a thing to dump our sun at dawn
    Into our western waterway and silt,
    The arrogance of Tor and Mound and pond
10 To kill a cause for what all three have built.
    For long before the pond there came the cold
    And long before to Mars we shall embark
    And yet before the Earth looked young and bold
15 No planets hung or moved within the dark.

    Heat death of the whole wide world
    What happens when it all goes cold
    Been here before I been told
20 Back then Big Bang it. Waiting for the bangarang.

    Efficient causes helped as much as gas
    But neither physic could dissuade the night,
25 So cause was Caused and Thoughtforms took on mass
    When Being said, "nonbeing, now be light."

Explosions in the dark, in freezer -- Heat.
The nova now conception's cosmic scale
30   For neither nuke nor sperm from meat to meat
Could sire the seven stars that light The Vale.
You grew by gas, by plasma, arc, and fire.
35   Ye added rock and ring and icy flame
Encycling you as you're in your desire
Enclyning kindly primum mobile's frame.

Not spinning circlet in the Earthen crown,
40   But more as symphonies move men to tears
So moves the cosmic whole, a verbal noun:
Enclyning: dance to music of the spheres.
In wisdom, stature, quicken Comet Dire
As fire spinners take to circus rings:
45   Make story knots of orbit, frock from mire:
Monks from peasants dunked in thermal springs.
It never lasts, this popularity
That comes from giving all what all require.
50   A well that gives and gives wet charity
Will yet itself run dry and then expire.

Heat death of the whole wide world
What happens when it all goes cold

55   Been here before I been told
          Back then Big Bang it. Waiting for the bangarang.

          Bring me some heat in this formless void
60
          For as we humans grow, your sheep of sky,
          Your bi-elliptic transfer — shepherd's crook

          Escorts our heat to Mars, close hook and eye.
65   And then, with gardens planted, pruning hook
          That cuts away the dead and sends us out
          Till every planet teems with budding life.
          Each Tor and mound turned States from
70   eagle scouts,
          We've set our sights on you with drum and fife.
          Run out of pressure, wind, and geotherm,
          Once harvest tides and nuke and chemistry,
75   We'll have no other source to reaffirm
          Our gold extraction -- cosmic dentistry.

          Bring me some heat in this formless void
          Bring me some heat in this formless void
80
          Now first we scoop your fusion into ships

And drink your fever, eat your daylight whole.
Your heliosphere shrinks and atrophies
85 Until our Dyson sphere turns light to coal.
Inhaling power till we sail the stars,
We never stop to see your dying rays.
We treat your motherhood as if it's ours
Like gold or river: Sun made mayonnaise.
90 Entombed by greedy mouths, you die alone
A death by suckling -- sustenance we leech.
Your breasts make nectar from your soul and bone
Until mind, breast, and ghost shades.
95 Overreach.

Heat death of the whole wide world
What happens when it all goes cold
Been here before I been told
100 Back then Big Bang it. Waiting for the bangarang.

My fellow men have left to eat the stars
But here I have returned to Sister Earth
105 Where Greenwood burrows tunnels in the dark
To bury still the ones who still give birth.
And there I look up to the rusty hull

That once engorged on lights and heats and
110   weights,
        I hear the vulture, crow, and laughing gull
        Rejoicing that we stilled what animates.
        But hulls in Greenwood bigger than the corpse
115   Still testify to metaphysic hopes.
        We build our shrines of marble in our parks,
        Why can't we build a tomb for telescopes?

        And so I led the mourners to the dark
120   To build a catacomb so yuge and bold
        That all mankind might pack their bags, embark,
        Return to homeworld left now in the cold.
        The Dyson sphere we reinforced. We built
125   An astronomical fountain and pond
        Where grows great world trees there within the silt
        And testifies of once when dark birthed dawn.
130   There in the womb of worlds we wept. The heart
        Of cause from "*Cause*," of Forms at "*Be*" amass,
        We long for once again. We pray: restart

135   While kneeling on the Tomb of Worlds's grass.

          Heat death of the whole wide world
          What happens when it all goes cold
140   Been here before I been told
          Back then Big Bang it. Waiting for the bangarang.

Rash Vows

I promise I am not a practicing Catholic,
But a renegade Protestant, ready to fight.
And yet I doubt.
                    Youth are walking
By the west wing windows in the Newman
Catholic Center, courtesy NYU.
They look inside: you learn from their faces
The thoughts they would hide. Thimblefuls
of Sehnsucht--

What warmth there, what's the light?
Free great books, free coffee,
From whence comes that piano, from where
this singing?

Their hands now hold a hollow circle
    Of storefront window, staring and mouthing,
Fogging the glass. Fearing The Mass
When they notice the cross and the naked body,
They all say, "Oh," and umbraged leave.
Mumble of abuses they mark as sins
    And crimes against thoughts curated for their minds
By that moral law made by Rome.

I think I am not a thing called "Catholic,"
But a devout Protestant, dying to fight...

The planter in the tea room playing the theme:
Greenwood speaks of growing things,
Of deeper wells than doublethink.
Its vines reach the vinyl and tiles
To make an arrow that in Morse speaks:
"*Keep to the old, kid, the old roads*
And you'll find your way, your future back home."
And the old servants of the secret fire --
Embers of the ages, (eld smell: vanilla),
Lining the oak lanes in the walls:
She calling me, shaking and fevered,
Banished child of broken Eve,
Queen of Greenwood, the quick, and the dead.

Am I at practice? Eager to be Catholic?
What is left of our weary Protest?
What but five weary centuries
Of bitterness and loss, too broken to yield:

"Bless us Father, we brothers have sinned."

55   "Years?"
               "Five hundred."
                      "Since your--"
                             "--Last confession."

LET ME BE HONEST

Can I confess all I'm feeling
To you, my stranger? Yesterday's
Observation of empty bowls
In the sky over Third escapes my lie
Detector's needle -- tinged by white,
The wet grays and wrought irons
Seem deeper, the snow capped
Mouldings and curbs. Minor adjustments
To urban environs eat at the way
We all think of this wild city:

Cool the shitsteam in them capped grates,
Orange pipes ease until clear,
Color us with the pure, calm down now
And sit in the hewn seat, carved pew
(*Pew pew, click, pew* and then *bang*)
Escape the holdup, scry for peace.

Rest here, child. Ready be,
Ready to be, ready as bee,
Ready be. Right is easy,
Virtue the quick, viable option.

Snowfall snaps the slick mirage
Of jaded careers: junk gilded.

Happy Days Diner

In the Happy Days Diner all the benches
Are blue sparkled -- boat metallic
Like my father's lures for fishing bass,
Like the Ranger he always really wanted.

In their window stands a weathered planter
Filled with the fire of fifteen vines.
Offshoots of The Plant That Ate Dirty
Socks and Seymore's. From Shop of Horrors.
You wonder about monsters and their weird children.
Or I do, at least. For evil is a sickness,
Boethius says. Evil can be cured.
For monsters, to Romans, admonish of dread
Cataclysm to come, a portent:
This is a monster. Things in the deep
Are merely one misery to come.

But the generation germinating
After the monster? Early childhood
Development varies... versions of rearing
Comprise fewer playbooks for the spawn
Of behemoth and horrors. So they hide
In the Happy Days Diner by the benches
Earning seven or eight bucks

An hour as dippers, easing the checks
From the pockets of patrons, pilfering Metro
30　Cards and cash. Skanda, the owner,
Raises them like his own, remembering not
To teach his own to take from the patrons.
"Sock Eaters steal, not us."

SONNET OF A SIREN'S SORROWS

The other ladies envy how I look:
my sea-through linens, white made light by mist,
my sun-bleached hazel hair, my body's book
Read right by now-dead sailors. How I've missed
The men who came to me, who heeded songs
I sang form-fit, an ear apiece: a dirge
For Dirk, a hymn for Henry -- right or wrong --
That steered their ships to smash upon my ridge.

Girls: envy not my slaying (*lust by hope*),
My Sehnsucht seems too much for men of skin.
For I desire Desire behind desires
While they desire not longing, but to grope
At straws of puberty as if to win
The Love of loves by burning Fire with fires.

Gothic White

Black boots and a button down
Have faded in the fury of a fountain washer
And dryer combo. Dread metal
And buckled shirts and belts of leather
All bear this un-tanning, embers in the dark.
White feathers worn by the outer
Wear itself. Wash, sunlight,
The daffodil stain, dandruff in fall,
And lily petals lingering in the seam...

Weird weather awakens her dread:
The hope of healing, the heather in crag,
Her leather stops lightning and bolt,
Charcoal on the marble, charcoal on the pulp,
pulp fiction and Pulp Fiction
In her black denim back pockets.
Why is she here? From whence came she?

Perhaps the Goths hold court in
New York City out of the need to feel
Gritty and grey, grown in the sewer.
But even in the sludge, embers awake,
Seeds sprout in the silt and a tree
Grows beneath Greenwood Heights,
Left by the graveyard, lingering light.

Gothic white. Given by the light:
How even Shelob earns her silk
By feeding on the good, her fellow beings.

The First Goths fired their cathedrals
With torches in the teeth of terrible goblins,
The gargoyles whose grins flare,
And illumine the marble, light the white
Of Chartres' stone on a Sunday morning--

--That has gone grey. Grates of smoke
Soot scarred it sable when the revolt
Of industry ate it. Even Rome must
Needs washing, now and again,
And the Chartres' stone on a Saturday evening
And the Black boots and a button down
That have faded in the fury of a fountain washer
And dryer combo dread both
The greying smoke, the greying feathers
And weird weathers of the awakening city.

Rewhite the stone. Rewrite the tome.
Blacken thy backpacks, thy bone and shoe.

55   The darkness isn't dark to Deity, really.
     It's more moth-eaten, more derivative,
     a second-hand store thing.

IRISH HUNGER

    Bronzed booties in the bathroom at my mother's
    Gave me the idea: got gold bouillon,
5   Coins, old chains, and a cauldron of sorts --
    Something meant for a science major --
    And lit up a fire on my living room.

    To the leprechauns we look and hope,
10   We Gælic run aground from caves
    In riverland rustic towns,
    We look to the greedy little tropes,
    The stereotypes stripped of racist
    Memes the culture calls "mainstream"
15   And "white" when we can't weather the crashes
    Thanks to genocide, thanks to England,
    Thanks to our Yiddish thoughts rejected,
    Thanks to the deaths of thistledown
20   Natives and Roma near here --
    Little Egypt and your little tropes,
    We little trolls, lugging gold.

    The fire is eating my favorite books.
25   I have brought an eight-ton cauldron
    And dumped gold in its dark bowl.
    No rainbow, just a nice pot

Of gold at the end of great peoples,
Five of them and feverish
From sweating out the swelter of whipping
We who prop winning classes.
I dip junk in the dread waves:
A shepherd's crook, a shackle from when
The wagon wheel I've whelmed with gilding
Was retained by migrant traffickers,
A ledger book of a lawyer (Jewish),
The things the culture thinks is trash,
We ones they call white trash,
Baptized in gold, brightening immersion,
Unwhitewashed, unworthy
Of privilege and power. Prayers for the keepers
Of the pawnshops and attics who pile high
Keepsakes for mothers, kinda like mine.
How many booties hardened by bronze
Were worn by children whose wild hopes shall
Never be known by negligent fat cats?
How many booties hardened by gold
Belong to lost little boys
Dead in the womb, dead on arrival,
Dead cause they got diddly for being
Born white trash? (Bronze statues
In Boston's downtown don't count).

THRENODY FOR GRANNY

4 A.M. I rise unresting
As the deer at dawn.
Mind on images arresting:
Mother, Amazon.
From its storehouse sobbing loosed:
Dread alone had bound
It to the tree of Death, a fruit.
Wished it: *never ground.*

She: bacon's morning herald,
Frying turned to war.
She: granddaughters her emeralds
Bankrupt giving shore
From Indiana lakeside --
Spite and malice rounds,
Marlboros and Fascination,
Pitch black coffee grounds.

You think the grave will hold her?
She the bane of bats?
She whose voice is morning thunder,
Tower shields for hats?
What great causes she gave grandsons
Sleep for now in Christ --
Hospitality and ransoms,
Ham and melon, sliced.

She is nearer than our words
Wasted on her now.
Near in thunder, coffee, birds,
Darke Fair's cane and sow.
Had we but a little faith
We would see the cloud
Of witnesses now real, not wraiths,
Shining hind the shroud:

Next to Patrick, Frank, and Paul
There sits a little girl
Who never lost her voice at all,
Whose hair has kept its curl.
She who bore our world in womb
Now younger, holds a hand
That holds the gold and cross and tomb
And every grain of sand.

Presents soon will rise high tide
Piling round the pine
That roots the world's Christmastide.
Her pictures wrapped and twined.
The Word unknown, unspoken
Knows now, speaks to us:
His great crossword unbroken.
BIC gripped by charlotte russe--

Her lady fingers filling
Blanks between the blacks.
New songs unknown by Dylan.
(Her view parallax--
She sees our objects closer
Than even we can see).
She hears the great composer's
Songs of victory.

Now she knows the Hence and Hither
From Whom all has gone;
Sparrows fall, lilies wither,
Yonder known by Yon;
All the Want behind her wants,
Longing known above;
Knows if love be want to wander
wandering to Love.

Some men think she waits ahead
Cheering at The End,
Some men think the sleeping dead
Will bolt from Heaven's pen.
But good men know human soul's
Naught without some bone.
Her body, mind, will sprout with others
From what Word was sown.

That Word, for her, on white stone
Her true name is her key
The Locksmith holds, unlocks her heart --
Each person's mystery.
For there was never one like her
Nor never will there be
Mother, Daughter, Sister, Soldier.
Sally forth, Granny.

See she has one more granddaughter
Courtney up above
Yet to taste her dunkey eggs,
Feel her ursine hug,
Yet to ride Durango runners,
Smell her Shalimar.
Courtney must catch up with Granny,
Then they'll pack the car:

For there is one Eternal Summer
Yet within our reach
Where Granny, Courtney, others wait
On Indiana Beach.
There the ski boats need no gas,
Kiddos cut the fries,
Corn hole tourneys last and last,
They never close the rides.

Gilded Beach Trash

There exists a woman who walks each
Morning before commuting to Murray Hill.
She leaves large living quarters --
5 Housing projects -- holding a bag
Of breadcrumbs and seeds. Brighton has the same
Beach boardwalk that bikers ride
To Coney Island. Coming there,
10 Sustenance she scatters and seagulls -- a tornado --
She conjures quick, clean as feathers
And rice in a funnel -- enriched plovers --
Lit by glass leavings and shards
15 Turned to diamonds, tears, and mirrors
By the rising sun, rendering gold
The abandoned boardwalk, boozing stone -
A yellowbrick yearning for young walkers --
20 Can toilets turn to timeless things?
Sanctified by the sun's sacrament and his rising?

A sunbleached subway map
25 Like some set piece saved for a My
Fair Lady Longbeach reboot or
At Brighton Beach barely whispers

"Maybe they might," marked by a circle:
Man, you're here. Meet me at the
30   boardwalk's
Chessboards, now abandoned by the locals --

Russian chefs and rising stars
In the carnival life, cut out for
35   The brewing of beer -- barely a tourist
By the abandoned colors and broke down rides
Of Coney Island, cleanly lit
By Brighton Beach's blazing star.
40
Grass grows. Greenwood shows
Up for the morning, Dover sends a challenge
To the D-line's dread metal,
Tufts in the sand. Teeming clover
45   Sweeps away swaths of stone dust.

There lives a lady who leaves feasts
In the morning, then commutes to Murray Hill...

Books Bear the Rose

Books bear up the bottom of the Rose
Reading room. Right in the middle
Of Bryant Park's perfect lawn.
Beneath the oaks, the old tomes hold
The weight of movies in the walking park.
Literal that may be -- literary pillars --
Books bear up the bottom of it all:
The towers and times, the tiny corner
Of the leaning table, the tip of the spear
And the pen which trumps the piercing ones.
Books uphold the water fights,
The waking nights of love working.
There's a broken TV in the Bronx that sits
On a stack of books plucked from the beams
That bear up the bottom of the Rose.

New Neighbors

This green haven I know
Bears evidence of new neighbors:
Maybe I should bring some flowers?
5   Welcome them to their new digs?

Twenty-five muddy patches
I saw on my ascent to Samuel Morses's pillar
No more graves left to rent
10
Will And Testament burials
Deeded to die here by family left
Worded to die not by Corona

15 It's louder in Greenwood
Sobs echo in barrowdowns
Children skip, enmasked, among the pink, the white
Tulip trees
20 Climbing bay and beech
Soldiers of sprouts. Spies of saplings. Tinkers of twigs
Tailors mending a tomorrow
Sewing seeds in a patchwork quilt.
25

Daffodil Farm

    Mr. Raver died on Sunday
    Left behind his daffodils.
    How he got them is the story
5   Told to minds to blossom wills.
    He had been a grey old pauper
    But for yellow in his hills.
    Mr. Raver died on Sunday
    Looked upon his window sills
10 Thought how grace will end in glory
    How we earthlings get sky gills.

Beshroud

Stone silks drape the spires
Memorial drapes: grey pall

5 There is a place where Sirius passes
Deep through the Minister's Black Veil

...between worlds is thinny,
Said Roland, who carried Black 13 across
10
Concrete clothing for the funeral furniture
Winterizing cemeteries for the end of the world

But the master of the house
15 Will return in Eastertide
And whip off the stone (quickens-to-silk).
Pluck obelisks, ripe carrots.

The roots of us go deep
20 Life's seed before harvest

EVERY PART, A PRAYER

The pen in my hand is a poem
Unlike the pen in my pocket's poem
My handy pen is prying precision
And smith tattoos on large sheets
Tribal justice, trinity's fount,
How I cannot see the ink
So it seems thoughts manifest in
Inked English.

The part of its poem's a prayer
The things and the peoples we write
Are speaking of things
Beyond all the things
The light hind the burrowing night
There isn't a crack in everything
But everything's a drill bit
And it'll bore you
Bore you
Bore you
Till it bleeds the summer son.

On Golden Pond

The shallows extend. Shorts, waist-high
Waves you will wade to half way
To the Isle of granite where old glaciers
5   Centuries of snow started to move.
Stable pontoons can skim the puddle
Take you where you thought to go.
But a man will meet many of you
On his dying dock, asking for a day
10   Of reminiscing with all the remnant folk
Whose family flees to the Golden Fleece
Of a pond in Maine, hoping for power
That comes in the Sabbath, then scurry away
To whatever cities eat rat food.
15   But the man's left in the lake's shallows.
Waiting for you to return to youth:
Waiting in the waters of Greenwood
The wood between the worlds where the ponds
20   Take you to other alters and ponds.
And a bell rings. And breaks you.
And you wonder why you left
The places glaciers paved your folk.

Where Treasure Is

　　I saw my buddy Mark and thought of shots
　　Of him and me upon a carpet red
　　I saw my buddy Colby, thought of plots
5　　Worth millions to producers (now they're dead).
　　I saw my teacher Jackie, thought of books
　　We'd write to both become full-self-sustained
10　　But when we tried to write beyond mere looks
　　Upon that purple sea we wrecked our brains.

　　My bride was picking pieces from the junk
15　　Arranged within an antique maker shop
　　And said, "This looks like mom... your brother... Jane."
　　The objects stacked -- her people, bunk on bunk --
20　　Her eyes are full of light: come folks from mops.
　　And mine are darkened: people turn to things.

HART AND THE MACHINE

It tells us something that the naturalists
Stuffed the most animals now extinct.
It tells us something that the naturalists
Dissected and vivisected the butterfly
And pointed and lied, saying,
"I now know this butterfly."
The dead one.

I would hate for them to get to know me.

It tells us something that every age has special evils.
We cruel, jealous, violent things.
We make anything and everything --
Any value or good vision or abstraction --
A chance to rape one another. And the land.
But these days, the worst politics, judgements, and cultures
Came from seeing Greenwood as a machine
And humans as technology
That wee bairn as biology
That lily as a gene
That orgasm as psychology
That orchard as sociology
And the politics and economics of beer. Or non-beer.

Did you expect something else?

30 If humans are walking factories,
If Greenwood is a robot,
Then families are dysfunctional.
Not merely messy.
They simply need *correction*.
35 And no reason and no moral offense can stop us
Taking it in for *repair*.
Or redesign.
Of course some who desire to heal the body
40 Mend the soul
Have abused --
Particularly while inflating their own controlling, domineering nature.
But in the ideal, at least we can hem the want
45 in
By dreading to offend sanctity
By fearing a breech in Greenwood's integrity
Trespass ye not the garden of the gods.

50 Not so for the repair shop which calls men and tree machines.
Gears have no holiness.
Oil is no mystery.
Mere proper or improper function.

And so:
'Scientific' racism
Social Darwinism
Eugenics
Inherited degeneracy for the sake of the prison industrial complex
Lobotomies will cure us
You must be sterilized
Children are inconvenient and must be taken out with the garbage
And the Third Reich
Who saw human and tree as biological tech to perfect.
And communist dictators
Who saw man and Greenwood as social and economic tech to rebuild

How to liberate a boy to grow up and be a dictator some day:
Step 1: remove his capacity for astonishment before the mystery of being
Step 2: remove his capacity for reverence before the mystery of being

The atrocities of the last hundred and fifty years

Came because we no longer kneel
in the chapel in the heart of Greenwood

To say otherwise is either blindness
Or propaganda from men
Who did not triumph over Greenwood
But rather learned to be one man triumphing over another man with Greenwood as his weapon.

This is what comes of fools who apply themselves to the
"Heroic" work
Of creating the future
Of dragging some higher or better human reality
From the stubborn dross of our "defective" species
Even if it means starting over from scratch in gene, race, society, city, money, or mind, etc.

I would hate for them to get to know me.

You cannot study men. You can only know a man.
Get to know me.

Get to know Green -- they recently proved trees communicate, which the Medievalists already know. Have you forgotten Ents?

Or:

Carry on.
I'll keep kneeling in these leaves and moss down
Here on the Greenwood chapel's marble
Praying your batteries run dry.

Brother Hudson

    The tide turned and terrorized the northern
    Shores of the Hudson, shimmering in the grey,
5   Overcast and embered by early light
    That silvers the slivers of the slave trade's
    Scions (waves), scouring crags
    And scrubbing off the moss of the scrying paver
10   That prophecies of our passing passenger train,
    That remembers many meditations bygone.

    The tide climbs and a tirade of salt
15   Fletches its watery firebrand darts
    For a river that's known for running both ways,
    Estuary of the east, Albany's Janus,
    Freshening and fresh, fertile and sterile,
20   Oyster and crawdad, ocean and lake
    Tidal borne. Oh tide bore
    To New York's gnarly heart
    And whisper wonder to its inner weather.

25   Has Queen Greenwood quickened your flood?

We watch you wander north, weathering the head
30   Of the fountain in the mountains, furious and giggling,
Going against your gaping flow,
Disagreeing with your dying selves.

35   "It takes a living thing to swim
Against the current," G.K. said.

Oh Hudson, oh herrings, oh happy salt
And sugarmint, surely you live.
40   Surely you thrive, sweet child of
Greenwood's gates, grown of the fountain
In the mountain and the merry making of salt
Beneath the deep of the barrows and oaks
45   Of the buried Brooklyn we can't bear to see.
Twinned and twining your twisted liquids:

Salt us and preserve ourselves in the flood.
Sugar our shames and sweeten our
50   bitterness.
Two cubes when the tyranny sours,
Ambushes us with acid rain.
A dash of salt when the drudgery of amusement

55 Keeps us apart, camps into arenas.
Acid for our divisions of entertained sugars.
Alkaline for forgetful ego (*you're contingent*).
Burn the city. Balm the country.
60 Bear us home, brother Hudson.
Bore us to tears, brackish honey.

Patina

How hard it is -- ever hear?
To muddy thy knees in major cities?
To scuff thyself on slate? Bark?
Hands bloodied with the hawthorn branch's
Rope burn, see? Red blood on
The brown hardened base of earth,
Fading to flowers, folding to moss,
All of it entering under the nails
Of your fingertips or the Father's cross,
Eastertide lilies earning their living
In the shit shining shelf of muck
That borders the bird bath of Greenwood:
Great pond and the glass castings
Of her fiery fountain, Fury of Waters.

When they chose the wood, was it a cherry tree?
Not oaken beams or elderberry,
But a stout-hearted, sturdy thing?

The holed palms of twelve pink cherries
Enloop the living lake water,
Disciples drinking dangerous fire
And bleeding their blood with the bath's graces.

When a puddle is Bethesda, pork belly the
Gadarene, greater towers
Than Babel being built round you --
Perhaps hardy horticultures --
The long-in-coming cherry's winter --
Speaks of the ones who spoke in tongues
In the wake of the risen wizard boy,
In the afttide light amber rising:
(*Tenebrae, Tenebrae*)
Oh Great Flood, irrigate,
Oh Rock of Ages wreck my ankles,
Oh Allergen choke, Infinite Pollen
asphyxiate my frame as friends did yours.

Oh Mud of Morning mutilate my knees
And slather me with thy patina of sanity.

LITTLE FLOWERS

A gilded lily grows in the park
Named Forest, nectar and germ,
St. Louis saves best for
Last looks in the life dimming:
French Catholics, friars embodied
In the flowers of Saint Francis and his jesters,
God's jugglers, *jongluers de Deiu.*

Greenwood's daughters have given themselves
Over to cities, each holding
Offering eaves, earning their keeps
And keeping their ferns for the claimed Gullies.
The iris eyes the eager sunlight
Of the well-lit vale and weeps for the mothers
Whose sons got shot by cocksure cops:
Certain a savior won't spring from the oppressed.
The palm paws at the powerless tin
Of shantytowns in Shinto countries
Where the vow to be poor is a vision of hope,
Rich descends rightly to serve
And the red carpet is a rictus leaf.

That the Rose of Sharon a rose is not
And yet it earns the yearning title
30   By being the love of brother Jesus.

Greenwood's daughters have gilded themselves
Not by the gilding (nearer my God
35   To Thee they cry), thankful and asking,
Praising and basking in the presence that fills
Each with sun and the image and word
Of water and soil, the witchery that upholds
40   Elemental undergirdings
Until the meaningless flowers are mighty and loud:
Little flowers loudly garbed
Better than the brightest, brazenest kings.

Guerrilla Sporefare

Over the Brooklyn Queens express
Took we the borrowed car.
Smog and the city fades away,
Snow globe of swirling smoke.
Forty or fifty exits pass
Greenery makes a noise:
"How have we passed both bought and grass
vines on the bridges poised?"
Greenwood has marshaled Ents in East
Rivers and wind and sand,
Most of the island East of Brooklyn
Is silent: surrendered land.
Come ye destroyers, vine and bud!
Come ye oh crumbling root!
Conquer by sower, water can,
Conquer by shit and soot.
Turn every roof to canopy,
Turn every wall to bark,
Turn all the sewers into springs,
Make of our sirens larks.
There on the beaches yet untrod,
There with the foresters,
Hear how the signals now grow dark.

See how the silence stirs...

A Family Restoration Project

    Oh banks of watershed we have travelled to,
    Conwego -- Current River smaller than you --
- how you
5   Flood high in Sandy, tropics, storming
        Waterline rising inside the carport

    Cold fishing. Amish building their waging
    Far over other side of the riverbed.
10   Green. Wood. You gathered people hither
        Arming them ever against the tech and

    Technocrats. Stabbing, bleeding them dry
15   from the
        Bamboo retaining wall that the widower
        Built overhead with teenage scion
        Over and over and overwhelming

20   Flash floods destroyed the cabins and porticoes.
    Mom died before the houses would hold in the
        Guests. Renters paying off her coffin,
25   Masonry, heating, and coffee mugs she

    Left. Now eleventh year since we wed and a

Child coming: houses we will anticipate.
Green. Wood ambassadors, we bring you
30   Songs from the city whose floods have reached you.

Sing we the song of sandbagging riversides
Sing ye the song of men who are sent by their
35   Girls downstream. Lights are never worth the
Losing them. One of the evenings we will

Meet over where the Conwego touches the
40   Long arm of the Susquehanna, the longest of
Cold water rivers when the steel and
Muskets arrived. How she Chesapeake mates.

45   Wakes ire of ghosts Atlantic and Albatross.
Green Wood, you haunt the waters of sailors and
Cold iron: teach us how to leave our
Mothers and wives and return to building
50   High walls for tempest: how the voltage
Shorts out when rivers rise and meet the
Great gods of rivers, meeting ghosts of
Old ocean fairy lands.

A Case of Nouns and Pronouns Denoting a Recipient

        Greenwood, there's a fire pit
5   Where we sit by the open
        Window doors, before bamboo
        And we think of you, groven.

        Greenwood, there's a beaver dam
10   Where I am, here with Echo
        My spaniel: bridging their traps.
        And the curves of maps beckon.

        Greenwood, how we paddled
15   In the saddle of canoe
        Murmuration overhead
        Am I dead? Hart. And flew

        Through Greenwood sparse in browning,
20   Chicken downing, strikes spray.
        The litmus is blue: a boy
        I've sired, joy in the shake

        Of womb in the Greenwood hue
25   Rocking lull of the Native
        Who sparked and brided and paddled,

Rode without saddle. Dative

His world: to, for, in, with, by
A lullaby for a son,
The whispered song begotten.
Crops from rotten. Just begun...

Oh Barren Womb

She climbed her way up Dover Hill.
On slackened grass she slipped and saw
The Ozark mountains, ate her fill
Of köfte. There across the falls
Another climbed the shale, a shawl
Went whipping off my neck her way.
She caught it. Blushed at me on wall:
"It is a boy," she said today.

A decade passed and still no child.
Walking through the cemetery
Greenwood weeps and the Greenwood smiles
Wet stone crumble, barrow scary,
Blooming catacombs. Now hairy:
Draw stick figures in dirt, I say,
"This suffices for a bairn, see?"
"It is a boy," she said today.

In nineteen hundred fifty-one
A derrick fell upon the Green
My grandad Jerry got his gun
To take it to the oil men.
But while he went, my grandma screamed:
"You cannot leave me here this way!"
Miscarried uncle Michael Dean.

"It is a boy," she said today.

30 The sugars still as Covid buries
Barrowdowns where Greenwoods play.
Her womb: it quickens, beats, and carries --
"It's a boy," she said today.

THE CRACK IN EVERYTHING

The books stack up like towers
They call, they beckon me
And reading them across the hours
I hear and smell and see.

I want to hear the wisdom.
I want to see the light.
I want to taste the fully cooked
And marinated Right.

By pen, I see the loving.
By poetry, the song.
By meditation every crack
In everything belongs.

For cracks all widely open
Into mouths like summer choirs
And even cold and stony things
Are lit: Empyrean fires.

HOLE AND HOLLOW

The hole and hollow hold the roots --
Hallowed be the hardy things --
For in the trough the incense burns
And ashes and embers order the soil
Nutrient rich in the naughty pits
Go the seeds of the Savior, shining in dark.

The hole and the hallow hold the roots
Of the morrow's morning, mighty bright
The sundry sun tree, simple hopes
Hallowed be the hardy things,
The seeds of summer, sundered and cold,
Burrowed and old, blacked and moldy
Like the mossy wells of midnight springs
Where peppermint sends shoots, appeals to nose
And in great holes green shoots are
Showing their shamrocks, shaping the luck
Of the deep dives: deity in the trench war
Where blood is wine, get ye bread from his skin.

The Chapel in Greenwood Tolls

    I wait inside the chapel
    Whose candles now grow dim
    And every window stained and framed
5   Alludes to thoughts of him

    But now the doors have opened
    And wanders in a breeze
    Of world unseen and grass untrod
10   Unsmelled till now the leaves

    I see the crumbling catacombs
    Whose bare earth cracks apart
    I hear the thumping of the dead
15   Who now have living hearts

    I hear the bell that's tolling
    Has tolled long after twelve
    It rings and rings and rings and rings --
20   Through stone and water delves--
    It goes on ringing over
    Every grave and blade of grass
    It echoes in the catacombs
    And every mountain pass
25   It wanders in the door with wind
    It shakes pew, altar, glass,
    It sounds like feasting, feels like tickles

Smells fried: beer and bass.

30　　I want to leave the chapel
　　　But not for chapel's leave
　　　I want to seek the tolling bell
　　　That pierced this chapel sieve:
　　　The light transposed to color
35　　Through the stories in the sills
　　　Is white beyond the window
　　　Is man beyond the hills
　　　Is heat -- no need of summer --
　　　Is peace -- no need of blade --
40　　Is God of wonder, thunder, wills,
　　　And pauper Christ's parade.

CHAPLET

    In pain the Presbyterian beheld
    That John -- that Calvin -- prayed his rosary.
    And so at Patrick's bought a chaplet dark
5   To pray as Calvin: banished child of Eve,
    Oh Mary -- hail -- and nunc dimitis, Hark.
    The chaplet fades with prayers of woe and weal.

10   For then the elders round them could invoke
    And then New Ark, New Eve, and Mother Queen
    Turn ebony-made-bead first into smoke,
    Then cloud above, then glory's gilded sheen.
15

    And now within the presence of his God
    The protestant is crowned with gold from sod
    A gilded vine, once held in hands as reeds,
20   Wreathes chaplet on his head from string of seeds.

The Kilns

I tracked mud into the Kilns the day before
We broke-and-entered C.S. Lewis's office.
This isn't a metaphor. It's a mindful
5 confession.
Two of them. No, three.

Arcadia

    600,000 in this city Green
    Attracted tours, beat Niagra Falls.
    For those who sought out old Arcadia
5   Had found its portal midst the urban dead
    Connected to the living town beyond.

    It is no urban desert, morbid place.
    Inspires colossal scale for parks of green
10   Within our cities, Central Park -- beyond --
    To showcase summers, blossoms, snows, and falls.
    Its wooden fence now buried with the dead,
    Reborn black iron: rise Arcadia.
15

    For iron holds at bay Arcadia
    And iron -- cast -- once fenced within the place
    Of lots to block live vistas for the dead.
20   They scrapped those for hard rain upon the green,
    The second World War where iron falls
    And lead to usher men to the beyond.

25   And now less iron holds in the beyond
    In this, the portal to Arcadia.

For now when moon returns and no soul's falls
The Fae longlivers travel through that place
30   That makes its stand in steel by stone and green
And summons forth the living to the dead.

The columbarium niches now the dead
35   Have taken over. Soon they'll rise beyond
The heights of iron in a wave of green
To doom and deem on York Arcadia.
A prototype: gave Auburn, Laurel place
In Cambridge, Philly, rural graveyard falls
40   Upon the Union. As Niagra Falls
Has Lady of the Mist, the Queen of Dead
Calls Brooklyn men to Greenwood, in that place
45   She calls the Greenwood people now beyond
Into the chapel in Arcadia
Whose green stained glass is long last truly Green.

50   As each one falls from city through beyond --

First dead, life after, then Arcadia --
A resurrected place from grey blooms Green.

What Moms Neglect to Tell Their Sons about Long Hair

It will tangle. Short hair brushes easy,
5   long hair hurts, so build your pain tolerance
nowish. That means grow your long hair early
here and now in towns and times where romance
lingers not. The grownups -- men and sleazy --
10 poke their fun at little children named Lance:
they forget how honor-bound and pleasing
men would grow it, bind it up: Earls of France,

Washington and Arthur, Socrates, Paul,
15 Jesus, Moses, Absalom's Fall, Samson:
why are razors manly? Men must need bleed:
manful virtue died: manliness is all
surface, all that's left, beardhair as ransom.

20 Long hair also protests, virtue sprouts seeds.
Aslan's mane? Come fuzz from tufts in the reeds.

A HALL OF TREES

A hall of trees, those knapsacks giant, left
By centaurs making water in the woods.
Their rootstocks bundled, burlap, twine, the
5 heft
Of heaven scrying, water witching goods.
They will be planted in the holes we dig,
But not the ones our bodies often fill.
These holes are made for resurrecting figs
10   And oak and bramble, hawthorn, cherry.
Skill
Is that which planters often lack or hone.
It takes a special person like my self
To scan my father's craft, turn plant to bone
15   And summon death from what grew live on
shelf.

My Sister's Dog's Birthday Party

    My grandfather greets the grey scrubbed
    Nurses and the night. Nicotine and smoke
    He ought to have inhaled, once you consider
5   How asbestos beats your bronchia and air sacks
    With C.O.P.D. "I could sleep on a nail"
    He says to my bride. She smiles and writes
    It all down for me. Ever wonder
10   Why we spend our summers in the sure blissful
    Distance of friends who do not keep
    The kind of spirit kindred that dads
    And grandfathers gathered and the great
15   pranks
    Of all my brothers, all my sisters,
    All of my cousins, and all of my mothers
    Surrogate or Caesarian? You show up to your
20   Sister's puppy's smash birthday
    Party and the people who please you there
    And they look long and they love and smile
    And you -- for one -- yearn to feel it,
    To know you are loved so near home
25   That it hurts to realize your house thousands
    Of miles away makes enough space
    For a handful of friends: home is where

Hearts are seldom for home is the rest
Of the heart whose hope is rewarded
With homecoming and happy, healthy tears
Of the joy of pajamas and jars of canned
Green beans that the grace of last
Autumn offered and opened spring
Brunch at grandma's, bounty and brethren.

When the Green Goes

When the green goes, England is green.
When other trees are eaten by browns
And the gummed grays of a great winter
-- The real film in a photo shop --
Mosses and molds make their way
Up the bramble, over the trunks
Till not even the naughts are abyssal
And death doesn't deem what is lasting
Doom for the fearless unto the Fae.

Even in the worst they waken the cold.
Even in thirst their magic thickens.
Even in hunger I hear the peal
Of trumpet thunder, timpani in the caves:
A lion's roar looking into the echo
Who wakens the wind. The wood stirs:

Greenwood is literal: greening dead wood.
And when it withers and washes away?
When the green goes, England is green.

The Comfortable Pleasure of Ascetic Vows

    We tend to birds of paradise
5   When robin breasts are redder
    Dig holes for gold below our dandelion sod
    Condition our air when year after year North Africans
    Dive in the Mediterranean instead
10   Common things evade us by way of over curious unneeded searching
    I read a study today: women in marriages
    Feel more, longer, deeper, compounded, and serial
15   Orgasms per week
    Than any other kind of woman in relationship
           Trust -- and wonder -- and therefore consent -- are castles, not cards.

20   My neighbor reads books about collective parenting
    While his children play on the floor
    Before him, waiting.
    "Yes, yes, the dog's barking. Did you hear them
25   testing
    The new emergency siren tower?"

Finding Greenwood

A place where the lighting is good
Where the fountain flows loud
Or where there is no fountain
But a pond at the least. With geese.

Shades of grey in trunks that fade
Into a background of gossamer light
Behind dark trees hiding mysteries
And from birdshit: rockbarms painted white

It takes little to make Greenwood here.
It takes a little time, a little effort,
A little legislative wyvern,
A little patience to bring back what
Machines break and concrete tombs.

It's hard.

But we can do it. We can. We can do it.

(we must...)

1,000 Each

    One thousand acorns apiece
    Is what it would take to waken the earth,
    To waken the wood and wind up the Ents
5   And pierce the concrete with peat moss and grass.

    One thousand acorns apiece
    For able-bodied over-twenties
10   To bury in the shit black silt of
    City streets: see how they sprout
    Fourteen trillion forest trees.

    Burr oaks in pockets, pin oaks in brick holes,
15   Red oaks in rock loads, spruces in rockets,
    Willows in Bay Ridge, bay figs in windows,
    Elms down in Wall, white oaks in Elmhurst.

    The trunks will tower through the cracks,
20   Barks breaking up the boardwalk footing
    Till Fifth Ave is a Farland Glad,
    Fairway from runway, free park from Free Parking,
    And the cars have nowhere they can call
25   home.

    I ride the rail back from Red Beacon.

Hudson heals the holy tide:
Salt from south seas the fresh river,
30   They mingle more: magma and spore,
Seed and city, shade and leaf.

Brother Sun sets beyond
Granite ridges growing 5'oclock
35   Shadow in the gold where I sometimes dump
The Sun at Dawn. Seed -- did you grab yours?
Come and seed. Come and seed.

40   Johnny? Oh Johnny? We're just over the hill:
Hold yer apples and heat our oven.

Hole: didja hew yours? Thrust: didja hump yours?
45   Spit: didja clock yours? Time: how'd you spend yours?
Soon rise up, sprout sisters:
Rehome our holy heathen swamp
That we, now fertile, may wake converted.
50
Rest now, restless waters,
For tuna and trout, timber and coal,
Kelp and crawdad to marry and settle down.

55 Joplin lamplighters fire, Narniad lamposts
    In the darkening Hudson's dead castles
    And riverdown valley rings of tomorrow:
    Bell Hammers in the cathedral belfry:

60 All is calm. All is bright.
    All is stone and ember and stem.
    Sleep. Sleep. Sleep to wake
    In Heavenly peace at heavenly price.

Greenville

"I went to Greenwood in the morn," I said
She said, "We're in *Ohio.*"
It's providential moment, more than space,
Greenwood Cemetery.
For Greenwood is *right here.*
For Greenwood is *right now.*
It takes a little barefoot walk
Out your front door or doors, down the block
You will hear the waters.
Feel the down of flocks.
Strike zone dirt and mushroom musk
And graves of gone befores,
Climbing trees, climbing vines,
The place where Fae is blooming.
We all now live in urban deserts
So oases matter more:
Seek the well,
Knock on the chapel,
Find me in the tall grass crouched for you.

I went to Greenwood today in Salem, Illinois.
Little Egypt's Bryant Memorial Park.
Yesterday I went to Greenwood in the Boston Commons.
Greenwood in Homer Alaska at dusk.

Greenwood in La Verna's musk and chill at dawn.
30   Greenwood clothing Black's Beach
Greenwood stripping the Swedish clean and celibate

And the Greenwoods underground
35   Where time and space and cities're bound
Waiting to rise Rivendales,
Reminding us that once we had no rural cemeteries
For everyone was buried in a country
40   churchyard.

FIVE GEESE ENGORGING THEMSELVES

The five geese engorging themselves
On the grass that grows from the graveside plinth.
They will take their treasure and travel to shit
All over your town. Only remember:
They could be stone. They could be statues
Of geese on a grave or a gilded tower
Whose memory is motto, logo.

One day, even these Canadian Demons
Will no longer have leave or welcome.
Even the mosquitos will go from quick to dead.
And you will long for a Greenwood lakeside,
Shout-cry-beg for one more shoe in their shit.

Bio. (you know, the koinh word for life)

Lancelot Schaubert has authored 14 books, 15 scripts, 40+ stories, 30+ songs, 60+ articles, 200+ poems, and a thesis for markets such as MacMillan (TOR), The New Haven Review (Yale's Institute Library), The Anglican Theological Review, McSweeney's, Writer's Digest, The World Series Edition of Poker Pro, Standard Publishing, and the Poet's Market — most recently his debut novel Bell Hammers.

He has ghostwritten and edited for NYT Bestsellers like Tim Keller, Brian Jennings, wrote the book proposal that sold Dr. Mark Moore's thesis (University of Prague) to TNT Clark, wrote copy for large international nonprofit orgs and companies, and has served as an editor for bestselling fantasy authors Juliet Marrilier, Kaaron Warren, and Howard Andrew Jones for the anthology Of Gods and Globes (not to mention work as an senior editor / producer for The Joplin Toad and Showbear Family Circus).

As a producer and director-writer, he co-reinvented the photonovel through Cold Brewed with Mark Neuenschwander. That work caught the attention of the Missouri Tourism Board, who commissioned them to create a second photonovel, The Joplin Undercurrent; he also worked on films with Flying Treasure, WRKR, etc.; helped judge the Brooklyn Film Festival and NYC Film Festival; and he wrote, produced, and performed the symphonic novella All Who Wander. Spark + Echo selected him as their 2019 artist in residence, commissioning him to craft 8 fiction pieces that illuminated Biblical pericopes. He lives to help others make what they feel called to make: to that end he has raised over $400,000 in the last seven years for film, literary, audio, and visual arts projects as an artist chaplain.

He lives a block from Greenwood Cemetery.

www.ingramcontent.com/pod-product-compliance
Lightning Source LLC
Chambersburg PA
CBHW011502220426
43661CB00036B/1456/J